Raspberries and Relevance:
Enrichment in the Real World

Raspberries and Relevance:
Enrichment in the Real World

compiled by

Linda Hoffman Kimball

CFI
Springville, Utah

ISBN: 1-55517-800-6
e. 1

Published by CFI
An Imprint of Cedar Fort Inc.
www.cedarfort.com

Distributed by:

Typeset by Natalie Roach
Cover design by Nicole Shaffer
Cover design © 2004 by Lyle Mortimer

Printed in the United States of America
10 9 8 7 6 5 4 3 2
Printed on acid-free paper

Library of Congress Control Number: 2004110391

Dedication

To the Exponent ladies and the Midwest Pilgrims, sisters all.

LHK

INTRODUCTION

We are beloved spirit daughters of God, and our lives have meaning, purpose, and direction. As a worldwide sisterhood, we are united in our devotion to Jesus Christ, our Savior and Exemplar. We are women of faith, virtue, vision, and charity who: Increase our testimonies of Jesus Christ through prayer and scripture study; seek spiritual strength by following the promptings of the Holy Ghost; dedicate ourselves to strengthening marriages, families, and homes; find nobility in motherhood and joy in womanhood; delight in service and good works; love life and learning; stand for truth and righteousness; sustain the priesthood as the authority of God on earth; rejoice in the blessings of the temple, understand our divine destiny, and strive for exaltation.

Relief Society Declaration
Presented by President Mary Ellen Smoot
General Relief Society Meeting
25 September 1999

Sister Mary Ellen Smoot, General Relief Society President from 1997 to 2002, said, "The declaration reminds us who we are, and Home, Family and Personal Enrichment night has been set aside to develop these skills."[1] With the changing of the name of these midweek meetings, formerly known as Homemaking Meetings (and before that "work meetings"), our leaders have sensed the Church's growing pains.

---

1. Mary Ellen Smoot, "We are Creators" *Ensign*, May 2000, p. 64

Eager for increasing relevance in an expanding church, the Relief Society presidency has said, "The focus of these meetings is to help sisters build spiritual strength, develop personal skills, strengthen the home and family, and serve others, while developing bonds of sisterhood. . . . As the Church moves forward, we sisters need to move with it. We need to make sure the challenges of living in the world will not keep us from what matters most. Home, Family and Personal Enrichment meetings will help us focus our efforts. They will help us become better disciples of Jesus Christ."[2]

Aware of a disconnect between monthly "'homemaking meetings' where craft-assembly projects and leisure-time pursuits have—in many areas—upstaged the real purpose of the gathering," Sister Sheri Dew, second counselor in the General Relief Society Presidency until 2002, speaks ardently on the issue. "The bottom line is, there are lots of sisters . . . who don't really feel connected to Relief Society. It's a generational thing. We've had 20 years of the three-hour block (of Sunday meetings) and now some of our . . . sisters see Relief Society as a Sunday class, rather than as this magnificent organization for women."[3]

Sister Dew's energy charges us to examine the purposes behind our midweek gatherings. "Relief Society['s] . . . express purpose is to help sisters and their families come unto Christ. In that spirit, I join . . . in declaring who we are and in rejoicing in the

2. "Home, Family, and Personal Enrichment Meetings," *Ensign*, Sept. 2000, p. 70.
3. Carrie A. Moore, "Relief Society looks beyond leisures", *Deseret News*, 1 October 1999

announced refinements in Relief Society's focus. We no longer have the luxury of spending our energy on anything that does not lead us and our families to Christ. That is the litmus test for Relief Society, as well as for our lives. In the days ahead, a casual commitment to Christ will not carry us through . . . . Sisters, this is a call to arms, it's a call to action, a call to arise. A call to arm ourselves with power and righteousness . . . A call to live as women of God . . . ."4

Home, Family and Personal Enrichment meetings will help us focus our efforts. They will help us become better disciples of Jesus Christ

---

The new format for Home, Family, and Personal Enrichment meeting ("Enrichment" appears to be the favored shortened name) is not vastly different from Homemaking meetings of the recent past. Current Relief Society General President Bonnie D. Parkin knows there is new vigor required to meet the lofty goals of building spiritual strength, developing personal skills, strengthening home and family, and providing gospel service. On this topic she says:

Home, Family, and Personal Enrichment meeting requires more connection to the Lord than ever before. It requires us to know—truly know—our sisters and their needs and then seek, receive, and follow inspiration to meet those needs as a sisterhood supporting each other.

---

4. Sheri Dew, "We are Women of God" *Ensign*, Nov. 1999, p. 97

When we struggle with Enrichment night, when it is not working, we need to evaluate whether we are simply checking off assignments or actually incorporating charity in our responsibility, and whether or not we are receiving divine direction for the program in our ward. In essence, as leaders we must be far more spiritually in tune with our sisters' needs and the Lord's desires for meeting those needs.[5]

Sister Parkin has high hopes for these meetings, which begin with a 15 minute spiritual lesson, followed by 60-90 minutes of activities. She says:

Home, family, and personal enrichment should add to each sister's resources and strength; it should bring sisters together to be sisters and enhance their commitment to live the gospel. In order to accomplish this goal, the evening should offer classes, discussion groups, and hands-on experiences that teach applications of gospel principles, keeping in mind the varying ages, family needs, circumstances, and schedules. Enrichment evening activities should place less emphasis on presentation and more emphasis on practicality and discussion.[6]

While our Church leaders renew and sharpen our focus, emphasizing "coming unto Christ" at every turn, they also underscore the need for

5. Bonnie D. Parkin, "Home, Family, and Personal Enrichment: A President's Message" www.lds.org, January 2004

6. Ibid.

"developing bonds of sisterhood." Does this new emphasis demand a Church-wide "cold-turkey craft withdrawal?" Not necessarily. There can be more going on in craft assembly projects than craftiness. Our leaders acknowledge this. Some sisters have been known while making crafts to bond hearts tighter than the super-glued ornaments they create. In every case, local leaders are to assess needs, interests, and relevance. In our growing community of saints, while some Enrichment nights might include cookie making or sewing instruction, there can be no "cookie cutter solutions" and no "one size fits all" answers to the challenges of our day.

> *The focus of these meetings is to help sisters build spiritual strength, develop personal skills, strengthen the home and family, and serve others, while developing bonds of sisterhood.*

The General Relief Society presidency suggested in 2000 that "the change has provided an opportunity to evaluate what has been done in the past and determine ways to encourage and inspire sisters in the future."[7] Now that the Church has had a few years to adjust to the new name and focus, how are we doing? Have we responded to "the call to action?" In this volume, sisters from varied life experiences and Church circumstances probe these questions with humility, humor, and candor. They share experiences from the present and the past which have colored their views of Enrichment or Homemaking

7. Relief Society General Presidency, Ensign, Sept. 2000, p. 70

meetings. In some cases they provide practical tips and topics to try in your own ward. Other entries are poignant and heartwarming accounts of meetings that accomplished the most tender goals of the Relief Society. While some women offer anecdotes of "failures," with the hope that from their lemons *someone* can make lemonade.

Also sprinkled throughout are words of inspiration from the General Relief Society presidency. Those quotes will be attributed to the speaker as will the occasional song lyric or handout in an effort to give credit where credit is appropriately due. For the most part, however, the participants are listed only in this introduction to preserve their privacy. The order in which the entries appear is not entirely random; nor is it predictable. This is a forum for sharing, an offering designed to stimulate your own thoughts and inspiration, not force feed you someone else's solutions. So, pull up a chair, join this conversation with your sisters, and see what might enrich you!

Linda Hoffman Kimball
Illinois, 2004

Contributors:

Kelly Austin
Alyson Beytien
Debra Blakely
Sharon Brown
Claudia Bushman
Harriet Petherick Bushman
Patricia Bushman
Jeri Cardon
K Carpenter
Rebecca Clarke
Sally Haglund
Nancy Harward
Linda Hoffman Kimball
Lael Littke
Laurel Madsen
Marci McPhee
Carol Lynn Pearson
Berniece Rabe
Cyndy Richardson
Jana Riess
Ann Stone
Janet Stowell
Connie Susa
Ellouise Susa
Shawn Tanner
Stephanie Thomas
Lisa Turner
Ardith Walker

Home, family, and personal enrichment meeting requires more connection to the Lord than ever before. It requires us to know—truly know—our sisters and their needs and then seek, receive, and follow inspiration to meet those needs as a sisterhood supporting each other.
—Bonnie D. Parkin

Raspberries and Relevance:
Enrichment in the Real World

"I received a letter which posed some thought-provoking questions about home, family, and personal enrichment meeting. The letter read, 'Are we the only ones confused about this program? Can you help me catch the vision of this program? Why are we doing this if the women do not want it? Why is this meeting called home, family, and personal enrichment?' How many of you have ever felt like this most honest sister? The name 'home, family, and personal enrichment' is designed to communicate what this monthly Relief Society meeting can help us accomplish. The phrase 'personal enrichment' focuses our attention on the importance of first strengthening our sisters as individuals; then with that increased strength, they will be better able to build their family members, friends, neighbors, and community, with the ultimate goal of bringing each closer to our Heavenly Father and His Son, Jesus Christ."

—Bonnie D. Parkin

Tarnished and battered, the tin tree and wreath are my most treasured Christmas decorations. Forty years ago, my mother made them for me at a time when cutting up tin sheets into fanciful shapes was the rage at Homemaking meeting. Mama loved all the crafts and quilting she did at the all-day meeting once a month on Tuesday, with lunch served.

Our house was colorful for a season with the roadside weeds Mama and the other sisters collected and then dipped in buckets of different colored calcimine. Pictures made of shapes hammered into copper sheets adorned the walls, and ceramic, hand-painted shepherds and milkmaids marched along the buffet top. But what I treasure most of Mama's craft efforts are the quilts she and her Relief Society sisters made for my trousseau. Faded and thin now, they still adorn my beds.

I often wished I could make decorations and quilts like Mama did, but those crafty genes were left out of me. My attempts at the crafts of Homemaking Meeting had a long history of disaster. I burned myself with the glue gun, I drew blood with the quilting needles, and I perspired heavily as I stitched together quilt blocks, invariably turned the wrong way. Once, when we were making fancy Christmas bows, everybody got the hang of it but me. Finally in exasperation, the leader took my hands in hers and led me through the intricate turns and loops demanded. But in spite of my ineptitude with all things handmade, those Homemaking Meetings were fun, and I learned a lot. With plenty of help, I always left with something to beautify my home.

And now Homemaking has become Home, Family, and Personal Enrichment Meeting—what a mouthful—and sounding so much more serious and impressive. Yet the old Homemaking Meetings, while a bit heavy on crafts, taught us to honor our families and enrich our personal lives through the sincere attempt to create "a heaven on earth" within the walls of our own homes. While we stitched and glued, we also had lessons on homemaking and mothering. Our conversations as we worked often centered on our spiritual struggles and triumphs. That by-product is still a goal.

But I'm glad that making something by hand will no longer be an absolutely necessary part of every Enrichment Meeting. I'm tired of burning myself with the glue gun!

The Enrichment Meeting is the slender reed on which what is left of the traditional old Relief Society is balanced. This is where we may get the Visiting Teaching message to broadcast forth to our sisters. This is where "We Meet Again as Sisters" over a pleasant meal, where we have the chance to get to know each other as we did in the old days, where we feel the sisterhood we used to share before our short Sunday classes of lecturing and listening. This is where we bring our miscellaneous expertise, where we teach the skills that we have developed outside the Church structure. This is where we learn about handwork, crafts, civic involvement, self-defense, the arts, etc., topics which used to be part of our regular Relief Society curriculum.

Having "successful" Enrichment meetings was a constant challenge. As Enrichment counselor in my new ward I learned that sisters came from varied backgrounds and levels of education, had different interests and skills, and ran the whole spectrum of commitment to and experience in the church. I felt pressure (from tradition? from my own anxieties?) to make this widely divergent group squeeze into a format that had worked so well where I used to live. I constantly felt like the prince trying to squeeze the glass slipper onto the wrong foot.

Then I read the instructions given when the new Home, Family and Personal Enrichment guidelines came out. When I got to the "activity segment" it was all I could do to keep myself from shouting Hallelujah! Here's what it said—with my emphasis added, or should I say, the emphasis the Spirit helped me see:

> The counselor and the leader responsible for the home, family, and personal enrichment meeting should work with the class teachers to plan miniclasses and activities **that will be relevant and meaningful for the sisters in the ward or branch**. The **suggested** miniclasses are **examples** of skills that should be taught. **They may be adapted to meet the needs of individual units**. Leaders should be certain that the miniclasses adhere to the topic and teach skills—including homemaking arts—**that will bring love, harmony, spirituality,**

security, and stability into the home. **A variety of classes or approaches should be offered to meet the needs and interests of all sisters**.

I feel so much freer now—freer to access the Spirit on behalf of my sisters here, freer to be more like the Savior—willing to metaphorically wash those varied feet, rather than squeeze them into something that doesn't fit. I don't even try to quantify "success" anymore. But slowly, step by much-more-comfortable step, we're getting to know one another and appreciate each other and understand more about the unity the Lord wants His daughters to enjoy.

"Home, family, and personal enrichment meeting requires more connection to the Lord than ever before. It requires us to know—truly know—our sisters and their needs and then seek, receive, and follow inspiration to meet those needs as a sisterhood supporting each other. When we struggle with Enrichment night, when it is not working, we need to evaluate whether we are simply checking off assignments or actually incorporating charity in our responsibility, and whether we are receiving divine direction for the program in our ward. In essence, . . . we must be far more spiritually in tune with our sisters' needs and the Lord's desires for meeting those needs."

—Bonnie D. Parkin

There is no sister so isolated and her sphere so narrow but what she can do a great deal towards establishing the Kingdom of God upon the earth.
—Eliza R. Snow

[The First Presidency recognizes] that there are many single-parent families; there are other families where difficulties exist between husbands and wives . . . and other challenges which cause stress in families. [Relief Society is the] organization which can provide that ameliorating influence, that balm of Gilead to unite all sisters in the Church. The Relief Society is indeed a balm that unites us, that helps us in our families.

—Elaine Jack

I was thinking a lot about my calling as Enrichment leader and wondering about fresh ways to create miniclasses that support the spiritual message. I read Sister Jack's talk "Relief Society: A Balm in Gilead." It was so moving and motivating. She quoted some lines from the old hymn:

> *There is a Balm in Gilead*
> *To make the wounded whole.*
> *There is a Balm in Gilead,*
> *To heal the sin sick soul.*[8]

She spoke of the variety of ways we serve and help each other. She said, "Wherever we are, we can carry with us a reserve of our balm of Gilead and we can spread it around." From her words I gained spiritual inspiration.

---

8. Recreational Songs, 1949, p. 130

But that's not all. I got practical inspiration, too! I can't wait for the night when we'll have a class on "The Plants and Landscape of Jesus' Life." We'll have a soloist sing the Balm in Gilead hymn. I've even got thin little samples of the wood of the tree from which the Balm of Gilead comes from, as well as samples of frankincense and myrrh! We're also having a nurse in the ward talk about balms, salves, and herbal remedies. We'll eat scripture cake. Here's the recipe:

Scripture Cake

Ingredients: (Look up the passages to discover what the ingredients are. Some references include more than one item so make sure you understand which one to use.)

3/4 c. **Genesis 18:8** (butter)
1 1/2 c. **Jeremiah 6:20** (sugar)
5 **Isaiah 10:14** (eggs, separated)
3 c. sifted **Leviticus 24:5** (flour)
3 tsp. **II Kings 2:20** (salt)
3 tsp. **Amos 4:5** (baking powder)
1 tsp. **Exodus 3:23** (cinnamon)
1/4 tsp each **II Chronicles 9:9** (spices such as nutmeg, allspice, cloves as desired)
1/2 c. **Judges 4:19** (milk)
3/4 c. chopped **Genesis 43:11** (almonds or other nuts)
3/4 c. finely cut **Jeremiah 24:5** (figs)
3/4 c. **II Samuel 16:1** (raisins)

Cream Genesis 18 with Jeremiah 6. Beat the yolks of Isaiah 10, one at a time. Sift together Leviticus 24; II Kings 2; Amos 4; Exodus 30; and II Chronicles 9.

Blend the sifted ingredients into the creamed mixture alternately with Judges 4. Beat whites of Isaiah 10 until they're stiff; fold in. Fold in chopped Genesis 43; Jeremiah 24; and II Samuel 16. Turn into a 10 inch tube pan that has been greased and dusted with Leviticus 24. Bake at 325 degrees F until it is golden brown—about an hour and ten minutes—or until Moroni blows a trumpet, whichever comes first. Cool completely.

Burnt Jeremiah Glaze: Melt 1 1/2 c. Jeremiah 6:20 in a heavy pan over low heat. Keep cooking until it is a deep gold, then add 1/2 c. Genesis 24:45. Cook until smooth and remove from heat. Add 1/4 c. Genesis 18:8 and stir until it melts, then cool. Drizzle this on the scripture cake.

Let me tell you my adventures with poppy seeds for time and all eternity.

You can often find me at the bakery supply store getting basics for my pantry at wholesale prices. But once it backfired. Along with the standard rolled oats and yeast, I asked for poppy seeds to add a little variety to my homemade bread. I could get a whole pound of poppy seeds (about the size of a quart jar) for $4, almost the same price as a tiny box (about 2 ounces) at the grocery store. "We're out of the one pound size, but we have a ten pound bag for $10. Is that alright?" I did a quick mental calculation and realized I could *throw away* 98% of it and still save money over grocery store prices. (Not that I could have possibly thrown it away.)

My husband unloaded the car and brought in the bag, about the size of a paper grocery bag, full of poppy seeds. He's used to my food storage excesses and my resulting culinary creativity, but this was too much. "Now you've *really* lost it. *What* are you going to do with *ten pounds* of poppy seeds?" We made the obligatory jokes about opening my own opium processing plant, seeing if the seeds would actually grow if I planted in the garden nothing but poppies that year, and storing enough poppy seeds to last the entire Church population into the millennium. Then I started in earnest trying to use up 10 pounds of poppy seeds, a few tablespoons at a time. We had poppy seed rolls, lemon poppy seed cake, and poppy seed muffins, I started giving away plastic bags of poppy seeds to friends.

Then I realized it would make a perfect favor for our Relief Society birthday dinner. One sister had a wonderful poppy seed salad dressing recipe. We could serve the dressing as part of the birthday dinner and give each sister a gift bag to take home with the recipe and a packet of poppy seeds. We could make 120 of them, one for each sister in Relief Society. Even sisters who didn't come to the birthday dinner could get a gift bag through their visiting teachers, with a Relief Society bookmark tucked inside.

I set to work making vacuum-sealed packets of poppy seeds, copying the recipe onto yellow cardstock, and putting them together into brightly colored gift bags. It took several hours to vacuum seal all those little bags. I got about two-thirds done when the unthinkable happened—I ran out of poppy seeds. I thought it would be impossible to ever see the bottom of that 10 pound bag of poppy seeds in this lifetime, but it was true. I'd run out of poppy seeds, with about 40 packets still to make. I thought of taking a little from each one I'd done, but it would involve reopening all the bags I'd just spent hours sealing. I decided to go back to the bakery supply store and get just one pound of poppy seeds to finish it off.

"We're out of the one pound size, but we have a ten pound bag for $10. Is that alright?"

I thought, "This is like a horror movie—I'm drowning in a sea of poppy seeds! I just can't do it."

I went home and repackaged some of the bags. Sisters didn't seem to notice that some got fat bags of poppy seeds and some got skinny ones. The dressing was a big hit at the Relief Society birthday dinner, and we all had a good laugh over the five basics of food storage—wheat, honey, milk, salt—and poppy seeds.

Poppy Seed Dressing

Combine and chill:
1 c. red vinegar
1 to 1 1/2 c. oil
3/4 c. sugar
1 1/2 tsp. salt
1 medium purple or white onion diced
1 1/2 tsp. green onion, finely chopped
1 Tbs. poppy seeds
3/4 tsp. yellow mustard

Makes about 3 cups.

When I began my calling as Enrichment Leader, the Enrichment counselor, Sandy, was wound pretty tight. She was a perfectionist. A talented perfectionist. Her invitations were exquisite. Decorations were delightful. And the dessert table, well, it was delectable *and* aesthetically pleasing. No details were left untouched. But it was taking its toll.

I, on the other hand, am a procrastinator. I like winging it. I trust that if we plan and pray, it will simply fall into place. Usually it does. But not always.

At first I just filled in where Sandy needed me, not always sure why we were going to such lengths or spending so much time on what seemed to me to be minor details. To see the way it frazzled Sandy—well, it was just too much pressure.

So I started suggesting that we scale back. We could still provide a lovely Enrichment without quite so much "fluff." Since I couldn't quite yet get Sandy to delegate, I just took over assignments. And since she was very sweet by nature, she couldn't bring herself to criticize my feeble efforts at decorating and food displays.

But slowly Sandy began to relax. She liked sharing our duties. And so did I. We became good friends, the perfectionist and the procrastinator. She learned to let go, and I learned to arrange napkins.

That summer, suffering with a difficult pregnancy, I confessed to Sandy that I hadn't made reminder calls in months and lamented that I couldn't keep track of the assignments she was giving me. She laughed and said, "Oh, I'm so laid back as an Enrichment Counselor." And she was.

My life has been influenced by Work/ Homemaking/Enrichment meetings maybe more than I know.

In the 1940s my mother made a soap candle at Work Meeting which we used as a Christmas decoration. I was enchanted with how beautiful and real those candles looked. When I started teaching school I let my students make soap candles. Now almost sixty years after my mother first did that project I am still making soap candles with my first graders. When they proudly carry them out of the school room I see the same glow that I must have had when my mother came home from Work Meeting those many years ago.

As a young mother in the 1970s I loved

Homemaking Meeting. I especially remember making a quiet book. Each of my three children, in turn, played with that quiet book during church. Then one day I stuck that book in a box of other old toys the kids had outgrown. Twenty years later I was tending my first grandchild one weekend. Getting ready for church I frantically looked through that box of old toys and found that quiet book. Now my sixth grandchild is almost old enough to benefit from that eternally fun project.

Recently at Enrichment meeting a guest speaker spoke about personalities using the color coding of red, blue, white, or yellow. I am a strong "blue/white" and felt everyone else should be just like I am. Over the years I have been critical of one of my fellow school teachers who is extremely unorganized. That night I gained a new understanding of that teacher, realizing that she is a "yellow" and her strong attributes are being creative and fun loving. I realized from this presentation that she is as legitimate as I am. We're just different. Enrichment enriched my attitude toward all of God's children.

When I was a child growing up on the farm, my mother had a large raspberry patch that was her pride and joy. It produced abundant juicy berries through three pickings. All summer we feasted on those berries swimming in the thick cream provided by the cows.

Even with a large family, there were plenty

more berries than we could eat, so Mother started her own small business selling them, and soon they had a reputation throughout the county. People traveled miles to get a carton or a flat of Ida McEntire's famous sweet raspberries.

It was a lot of work to pick all those berries. I remember my mother—garbed in a long-sleeved shirt over her house dress, with a broad-brimmed hat to keep off the hot sun—toiling away hour after hour, filling her little berry buckets.

How on earth did Mother accomplish all she did? Even though she was spending hours in the berry patch each day, she was also taking care of her garden and kids, and cooking huge meals for Dad and the farm workers. What's more, she was Relief Society president!

And thus it was that once a month in the summer, the Relief Society sisters gathered in my mother's large, airy living room for Homemaking Meeting. Happily ensconced on the floor under the quilting frame, I listened to the talk and laughter as they worked. (No tied quilts in those days; most Mormon woman were adept at the tiny, perfect stitches required.) They made quilts for the trousseaus of one another's daughters; they made them for sale at the annual Relief Society bazaar; and they made them for families in need. Each one was a labor of love.

Sometime during the hours of quilting, the ladies paused to refresh themselves with bowls of freshly picked raspberries served with cream in Mother's best china, and with linen napkins to spread across their flowered dresses. From my snug hiding place beneath the frame, I heard their exclamations about the deliciousness of the treat, which they knew came from Mother's berry patch. I remember the prayers that blessed the berries, giving thanks for all blessings and acknowledging the presence of Christ in their lives. (Thanks to Mother and the Primary, I knew all about Jesus.)

More than half a century has passed since those long summer afternoon Homemaking meetings. They weren't called Enrichment meetings back then, but even as a child I recognized the rich atmosphere of sisterhood as the sisters of the Relief Society quilted, prayed together, and shared raspberries and cream served to them with love. When I go to Enrichment Meetings these days, I don't spend hours underneath the quilt frame, and I've not yet had raspberries as the refreshment, but I still enjoy the sisterly love and sharing, and the coming unto Christ that continues to be the foundation of Relief Society.

From the grocery store, bring home a couple of bananas, two quarts of pineapple sherbet, and one tin of frozen, sweetened raspberries. Let them sit in the bags while you put other things away, answer the phone, and deal with your family for 20 minutes. When slightly softened, put the sherbet into a large bowl and stir until it is smooth (but still frozen). Add the tin of the now slightly thawed raspberries, including all the juice. Stir until smooth. Cut two bananas into small chunks and stir those in as well. Put the mixture into a container, cover tightly, and put in the freezer. Let freeze until solid (several hours during which you can deal with the ethical question of how to respond when your delighted guests say, "Wow, you made homemade sherbet. This is really great.") The trick with this is to make sure the sherbet never really thaws or it will get solid ice crystals in it when it goes back in the freezer.

Having been in three city wards—as Relief Society President in one and Homemaking Counselor in another—I have seen some enrichment action, or lack thereof. It is the same few people who plan and the same few people who come. Often those who come are trying to support the people who plan. The sisters I've seen over the years in this area who attend are between 21-45, white, stay-at-home mothers who may be interested in the topics offered but also need a night out. These people usually have transportation. Requesting sisters to bring those they visit teach, a neighbor, or someone without a car usually didn't work.

In my experience, those who don't come to Enrichment are 1.) Single moms who may work nights, but if they don't, are helping kids with homework, fixing dinner, etc. They may have a car but no one to watch their kids who may be older than nursery age. 2.) The young single working girls who feel Enrichment is for the older women. 3.) Elderly women who may not want to go out at night. 4.) Professional women who may feel they don't want to take the time. They don't have to be there to present something, they may have no interest in the topic, nor do they want one more meeting. In one ward the African-American women usually did not come, and if they did, they felt pretty out numbered by the young student wives, despite our best efforts to welcome and involve them.

But beyond all my generalizations, here are some Enrichment Meetings that worked:

·Going to the food pantry
·Asking nonmembers/friends to do a cooking demonstration
·Mother/daughter quilting class
·Gathering up supplies for moms to have Nativity "dress-ups" for their children at Christmastime
·Having a craft day but giving what you made away to a widow or other member not in attendance
·Practicing '30s and '40s tunes to sing in a nursing home

When a ward not my own called to ask me to speak about Christ and the women of the Gospels at their Enrichment Meeting in December, I readily agreed. Christ's love and respect for women is a message I enjoy bringing to the sisters of the Church.

I had given my talk for my own ward's Enrichment night, but have to confess that I rarely attended these meetings because I had made up my mind I wasn't interested in what was offered and, besides, most of the women attending were young enough to be my daughters.

It was the same when I arrived at the other ward's Enrichment meeting; most of the women were young mothers, many with babies in their arms. But they greeted me warmly, and as I presented my talk, they were a wonderful audience. They listened intently and were full of thoughtful, intelligent questions and comments.

We continued the discussion about the Savior and women as we sat together afterward, eating cheesecake while they made little angels out of fine wire for their Christmas trees. Being extremely craft-challenged, I begged off, but I enjoyed the conversation and their spiritual insights.

The talk among us also ranged over myriad other subjects, including potty training. Quite a number of them were engaged in that serious endeavor, and since, once upon a time, I had successfully taught four little ones the art of the potty, I took enthusiastic part, while they listened respectfully (but skeptically) to my old-time methods.

As the evening wound up, my newfound friends presented me with several of the tiny angels to grace my Christmas tree. Bearing these and an extra piece of cheesecake for my husband, I felt the light-heartedness that comes from having had a good time. I'd found that the age difference between us didn't matter at all. We'd had fun together, and we had found common ground in talking of the Savior and of our children. At home, as I put the angels on the tree, I realized that I had indeed been enriched at Enrichment night. And I've gone to be enriched each month since!

During the two years that I served as Homemaking/Enrichment leader the focus and name officially changed. I realized as I reviewed my files from those years most of what we did were crafts! For almost two years! Not that doing crafts each month was so terrible; I liked it. It's sort of funny. For instance, one month the theme was "Nurturing Children," and we had a Mother & Daughter craft night or a Mother & Son craft night. When it was "Strengthening Families" we did scrapbooking and family trees painted on a plate (genealogy!). It's all about how you present it— marketing and advertising! I had certainly convinced myself that the classes we had went right along with the theme and were beneficial to the sisters. When I look over what we did, it turns out to be sort of like an index from the *Martha Stewart Living* magazine. Still, we did some fun things and, most importantly, I like to think that the sisters had fun, too.

Not long ago, a group of my best friends gathered in a hotel room in Chicago to begin a weekend celebration of our collective 60th birthdays. We had been friends for over thirty-five years, having met at church in Chicago. And what were we doing to launch this weekend of fun and furious festivities? We were doing a craft. In honor of "the year of the sheep," which is the Chinese zodiac sign of our birth, we were wrapping cut-out wooden sheep with various colors and textures of woolen yarn.

The irony of this activity was not lost on us. Most of us had eschewed crafts (perhaps with one exception, and her crafts were works of art), and in fact had mostly boycotted craft night at Homemaking/Enrichment meetings through the years. However, here we were sitting around a table, happily wrapping yarn, talking, laughing, and remembering other such moments in our time together.

Three of us had served on a Homemaking committee and had become friends planning such activities as learning to make bound buttonholes, cake decorating, making lingerie (i.e slips), and an experiment with some unusually ugly yarn flowers. As we reminisced and laughed about these and other projects, we noted that none of us had ever since become proficient at bound buttonholes or slip-making, nor if given the choice, would spend much time decorating a cake. What was clear is that those crafts had brought and bound us together. As much as we loved book discussions or good speakers or talent shows or exercise classes, the meetings we remembered most were the ones where we had the opportunity to talk, laugh, and work on something TOGETHER.

We were hungry for time to visit and get to know one another and something in our Mormon DNA mandated that we be doing something with our hands at the same time.

At some point in our Relief Society careers we have all taken a survey of some kind to determine what kinds of classes we'd like to see offered at Enrichment. As often as we have all said we wanted more classes on scripture study or parenting or equally valuable skills, the best attended meetings have historically always been those with craft projects. Personally, I don't want another hand-made item entering my house, but I love making service project items with my sisters; I love quilting; I even love putting together 72-hour-kits; but mostly, I love the time to visit. Thirty-five years of lasting friendships started in this way and we are wound tightly together as those cute yarn sheep.

I don't remember how to make Easter egg wreaths, but I remember waiting my turn for the hot glue gun and listening while a new young sister in the ward whispered to me that she was desperately lonely and depressed. She wondered if I would watch her two small children while she met with a therapist. If we hadn't been there together with the opportunity to talk, would she have had the nerve to call me? I'm convinced I wouldn't have been sensitive or perceptive enough to guess her need.

There is no sister so isolated and her sphere so narrow but what she can do a great deal towards establishing the Kingdom of God upon the earth.

—Eliza R. Snow

"Homemaking, Homemaking"

To be sung to the tune of "Matchmaker, Matchmaker" Music from Fiddler on the Roof by Jerry Bock. Lyrics copyright 1991 by Nancy Harward. For performance, use music from the original score and omit bars 71-106.

Homemaking, homemaking,
Make me a home.
Make it with glue
And Styrofoam.
Homemaking, homemaking,
What can I do
To make me the perfect home?

Homemaking, homemaking,
I must admit
I can't create—
Sell me a kit.
Give me a pattern so my home will look
Just like the one in the book.
I'm not that much of a knitter,
But maybe I could learn to crochet.
My friends say to try Scherenschnitte,
But I'm not cut out for that, I'm afraid.

Homemaking, homemaking,
Stitch me a stitch,
Quilt me a quilt,
Craft me a craft.
Last time I tried to my fam'ly just laughed,
So what should I try, after that?

Sister, dear sister!
Have I got a craft for you!
It's simple; it's cute!
All right, it's useless, too,
But it's a nice craft,
A good class—
True? True!
I promise that you'll love it.
You'll finish it tonight—
And even if you don't,
Some day you might.
Do you think that you can come?
Well, I'll try to get away—
But the laundry,
The dishes,
The ring in the bathtub
Can't wait another day.

Homemaking, Homemaking,
Weed all my weeds,
Wash all my wash,
Meet all my needs.
Homemaking meeting might be kind of fun,
But none of my homework's done.
A glue gun won't fix the plumbing,

And puff paint will not iron a shirt.
I think I'm fin'lly succumbing
To stress and disorder and household dirt.

Homemaking, homemaking,
Aren't you aware
Making a home
Takes constant care?
How can I make it if I'm never there?
So stitch me no stitch,
Quilt me no quilt,
Craft me no craft
With Styrofoam—
Tonight let me stay at home.

"Enrichment Nights"

To be sung to the tune of "I Could Have Danced All Night"
from *My Fair Lady* by Lerner and Loewe. New lyrics copyright by Patty Shelley Bushman.

Hey! Hey! I'll start my own crusade,
And tell the world how great this program is!
Yes! Yes! We shouldn't make them guess
Why we are ecstatic—now hear this!

I now can surf the net,
And make a crepe Suzette,
Enrichment Nights are great!

I wrote my history,
And traced my family tree,

My journal's up to date.

I quilt and sew, do tae kwon do, it's easy!
I pressed some flowers in seconds flat.

I cooked some wheat chili,
And learned calligraphy,
Enrichment Nights are where it's at!

I did estate planning,
Food storage and canning,
Enrichment nights are great!

I learned to caulk the tile,
Improve my domicile,
My home is now first-rate.

I harmonize and exercise with pleasure;
I know first aid and health care, too.

We still do crafts, you see,
But not excessively,
Enrichment Nights—oh, I love you!

I believe that Enrichment is or can be a blessing in our lives. At its best, it builds sisterhood and strengthens and enriches our hearts and minds, bringing us closer to the ideal of "sisters in Zion." I have experienced this on rare occasions and am still open to making the effort to attend when I think that some good can be accomplished by that effort.

When Enrichment was called Homemaking, I too often saw the painful irony of leaving a home that was always in need of my presence in order to "talk about" making that home a better place. Needless to say, talking is not doing, and I usually could not justify leaving the doing undone when I doubted that I would return home with much in the way of worthwhile knowledge, wisdom, or motivation.

I attend Enrichment now with the idea of using the time to get to know my sisters better. If the structure of the evening allows for that, I usually try to attend.

I have a testimony of and a passion for Christ-centered women of otherwise far-ranging backgrounds gathering to talk and enjoy each other's company. I find it wildly amusing that we work so hard to disguise these Wednesday nights. Why can't we just get together to eat and chat? Without a formal name and lesson would things deteriorate into gossip and gluttony? Are we so unsure of ourselves as women and sisters?

I have always enjoyed it when someone asks me where I learned a particular skill, and I can say, "Oh, I learned that in Enrichment." Enrichment should offer something that will "enrich" my life. My desire to attend is enhanced when I can learn something that is useful, practical, and can be incorporated into my daily life.

Enrichment isn't always convenient, but when sisters teach and help other sisters, it can provide a lifetime of little lessons that make our lives "enriched."

Soon after I graduated from college I moved East where my parents had just re-located. I didn't know any of the women, and they were all older than I was. I only went to the first Enrichment Night because someone was teaching how to make abelskivers. This is a Danish pancake that I first tasted when I lived in Santa Barbara, California. Our LDS neighbors up the street made them all the time. We loved them, but had no idea how to make them. When I went to this class the teacher made sure each one of us took a turn at the stove, so we would know how to make this tricky pancake. I went out and purchased the special pan and have been making abelskivers ever since—much to my children's delight.

✤

Every Thanksgiving, whether we dine at our house or a friend's, I always offer to provide the "nut cups." When I lived in New York City I belatedly showed up to an Enrichment Night where they were offering holiday decorating tips. The thing that stood out in my mind the most was the Turkey Day nut cups. I love them because they are so easy. You take a mixture of your favorite ingredients (at our house it's honey-roasted peanuts, candy corn, and Reese's Pieces), put them into a sugar cone, and lay them flat behind every guest's plate. *Voila*, their own little cornucopia. My kids now insist on being in charge of this tradition every year.

When we lived in Moscow it was very difficult to have Enrichment. We didn't have a church facility where we could meet during the week and all the sisters lived far apart. We generally met once a quarter and even then it wasn't easy. The most memorable activity was the one that was the most difficult to get to. It was February and there was snow and ice everywhere. I had to take several subways to a sister's apartment. When I reached the apartments, there were many buildings that all looked the same. I knocked on many doors before I found hers. But we made it—all eight of us— because this sister was teaching us how to make tortillas from scratch. That was a product you couldn't find in Moscow then, and we were all anxious to learn. I think those were the best tasting tortillas I have ever had because it took so much effort to be there. We were quite proud of ourselves as we left, still covered in flour, with our souvenir tortillas we each had made.

Enrichment isn't always convenient, but when sisters teach and help other sisters, it can provide a lifetime of little lessons that make our lives "enriched."

❧

I live in a ward and stake that is very diverse and short on resources, including leadership capabilities. I attend most Church activities with the attitude that I will be serving, rather than being served. If I expect to be "enriched," I often feel disappointed and then resentful that I have wasted my time. However, I am enriched and blessed by my service at church and by the opportunity to interact with women whose lives and backgrounds are delightfully different from mine.

In at least one ward, attendance at Homemaking meetings was deemed a measure of orthodoxy. That brought clusters of the pious and the grudging. The woman coordinating Homemaking meetings in that ward made it clear that she did not consider attendance mandatory. It was an opportunity, as Sister Virginia Jensen, former first counselor in the General Relief Society presidency, put it to "share sisterhood, to gain knowledge, to learn skills, and to increase testimony." When the pressure was off, happy crowds came.

I want more time devoted to sharing stories with each other and laughing. If Enrichment Night and Relief Society are to be our haven of peace and support in the world, does it always have to have "classes"? Sometimes Enrichment Night seems to be about making ourselves crazy trying to do more or feeding our vessels of perpetual guilt. Couldn't there be a few nights where we are devoted to learning about each other?

❧

For one Enrichment Night we were all given a brown paper sack to bring filled with something that represented us. We were told we'd give the item away to another sister, and that we should choose something others did not know about us— something like a recipe, a poem, or a favorite treat.

I felt self-conscious, young, and out of place as we sat in a large circle in the Relief Society room with our closed sacks on our laps. The president began by pulling out of her sack a large popcorn ball. She talked about how her favorite food is popcorn and how she'll take a "popcorn break" whenever she gets annoyed with life, and then detailed for us some very candid and funny moments of frustration. Then she gave the popcorn ball to me and said she admired how I was taking care of my children. Her reaching out to me encouraged me to share the contents of my sack—a packet of wildflower seeds—with a new sister in our ward who I suddenly realized probably felt younger, more self-conscious, and out of place than I had been feeling.

One mother of ten brought out beautiful illustrations that she'd done years before and told of how she was excited for the time when she'd be able to draw again, and gave a drawing to a woman she admired. A newly single sister brought a bag with plumbing supplies in it to show her newfound skills in taking care of her home. A Spanish-speaking sister brought a small matchbox with tiny items that represented the Book of Mormon, and bore her testimony in Spanish.

I did not plan on laughing so hard when I first entered the room. I did not plan on learning so much about my sisters in such a short time. It was an Enrichment Night where I was surprised to find out how funny and how down-to-earth the wonderful women in my ward were, and how much I had in common with them. It was a unifying experience.

This was no polished, proper Enrichment event. We held it in the gym. We had a large circle of chairs around a layering of mismatched vinyl tablecloths I had found in the Relief Society closet. In the center of this color-clashing covering was a black staircase, about four steps high, with a basket of eggs on the edge. No lace tablecloth. No stunning centerpiece. Just tablecloths, a staircase, a basket of eggs, and me.

To begin the lesson, I asked the sisters if they ever felt like their shells were too thin, if they ever felt like they were going to "crack." It was January, so holiday stress was still fresh on their minds. We were going to purge, I told them. I wanted each sister to come to the stairs, share or reflect privately on a major stress in her life, and drop an egg. (Always say "drop," not "throw," "smash," or "toss." They'll do that anyway.)

I started us off by sharing some stresses from my immediate family: a brother in prison, a family divided, my anger at the effect of this sibling's choices. Then I dropped my egg, climbed down from the stairs and waited for the others to join.

They were a bit reluctant at first, but they eventually shared.

Their trials and stresses ranged from the commonplace—too much company for too long—to the heartbreaking—rebellious children straying from the gospel. They dropped—or threw—eggs in a moment of catharsis. Some sisters didn't throw an egg at all. One sister dropped two. A single sister, who had already dropped one egg with the profession that she was perfectly happy, approached the stairs again and confessed she had been lying. "I am sick and tired of being single," she lamented, and threw that egg. Yolk was flying. The circle of chairs was barely big enough to keep egg from landing on the sisters.

Then I asked the sisters to create an egg-catcher. With another group of sisters, they were to take mundane household items—toilet paper rolls, tissue boxes, mateless socks, twine—and create a protection for the egg. As I listened to the drone of conversation from the busy workers, I removed the egg-covered top layer of tablecloths. Then we dropped again.

This time as we dropped the eggs, I asked the sisters what types of things in our lives provide protection to our shells. We covered the "Sunday School" answers: read the scriptures, keep the commandments. And then we really got serious: temple experiences, nature hikes, personal contemplation. My favorite moment was when a group of three sisters brought their contraption to the stairs. One stood atop the stairs creating a sort of pulley system with two sections of twine. The other two sisters worked the system by pulling and directing the twine to lower the device to the ground. The vinyl zipper case holding the cushioned egg didn't drop; it coasted gently to the floor. It was poetic, as was their description: "loving hands to guide, good friends to help, and the gospel to cushion our fall." I could have ended there, but I didn't.

I also made sure to have one egg-catcher that didn't quite work: the egg still broke when it landed. I ended with this device, reminding the sisters that sometimes, even with the gospel, our shells can crack. But the Supreme Healer can pull us back together, patch us up, and heal our shells. The Savior can do the one thing my object lesson could not: reconstitute that egg.

One of the best classes I attended at Enrichment was on depression. It was led by two sisters who deal with significant depression. One sister had been clinically depressed for years; the other had extreme bouts of bi-polar disorder. Since I was in the Relief Society presidency at the time, I knew the struggles they faced. When we tentatively broached the subject with them, these sisters were amazing in their willingness to share their pain with others. We had no idea how the other sisters would react to this topic. The room was packed! It was the most unbelievably loving, open, supportive environment I have ever experienced at an Enrichment Night.

Some sisters attended because of experiences with family members, while others were certain they had depression and wanted to find out what to do. Some sisters came to find out how they could support other sisters they visit taught. There was no judgment— only love, support, and sharing of knowledge.

Joyce, our beloved, soft-spoken former Relief Society president, was about ten minutes into her presentation on "Christlike Parenting" when Veronica strode through the rear door of the Relief Society room. Now it isn't unusual for people to arrive late for Enrichment Meeting, but Veronica didn't just slip in the door and quietly take a seat in the back like most latecomers do. Instead, Veronica marched right up the aisle toward the front and began screaming at Joyce.

"I hope you know you've ruined my life!" she yelled, her voice sharp with anger. "I thought you were supposed to be my friend! I thought I could trust you! Well, I was wrong, wasn't I? I can't trust you, and you're definitely not my friend. I hate you. I HATE YOU!"

Veronica had reached the front of the room and was gripping poor Joyce by the upper arms.

"Why did you lie about me?" Veronica continued. "Does it make you feel good to know that you have totally ruined my life?"

The outburst was so unexpected that we all sat paralyzed, sure that something should be done to stop this horrifying scene, but unsure exactly what that something should be.

Practically everyone in the room knew that Veronica's emotional state was fragile. She had been out of a job for nearly a year following an accident that left her in constant pain. We knew, too, that she was worried about her equally fragile teenage daughter. Some of us also knew that Joyce was Veronica's visiting teacher, and that Joyce had worked with extraordinary patience and compassion to help Veronica bear her burdens. No one could imagine what Joyce might have done to warrant such an impassioned attack, but neither could anyone decide how best to defend her without hurting Veronica.

Finally, someone in the front row rose and moved toward the red-faced woman who was catching her breath after another barrage of "I HATE YOU!'s." Just then, however, Joyce turned and calmly addressed the audience.

"How many of you have faced an outburst like that from an angry child?" she asked.

Then she turned back toward her adversary.

"Thanks for your help, Veronica," she said, her eyes twinkling. "I think Veronica deserves an Oscar for that performance, don't you?"

Veronica smiled and found a seat, while the class—with our breathing returning to normal and attention entirely focused—listened to the rest of Joyce's excellent lesson.

I have found that the very best Enrichment lessons are the ones that get the sisters actively involved and talking about their own lives. In our ward when we had lessons that were straight-from-the-manual lectures on gospel topics, people stopped coming. When we settled into a balance of hands-on activities, food, spiritual nurture, and fellowship, the sisters began looking forward to Enrichment again. In my experience, Enrichment needs to be something special, something warming, for the sisters to make the extra effort to come to church on a busy weeknight. It should be spiritual but not preachy or didactic.

The women who make decisions about Enrichment Meetings in any ward face tough questions and deserve our prayers and support. On their behalf at least, let's invigorate that dear Relief Society motto: Charity Never Faileth.

Years ago (in the 1980s) when I was Stake Relief Society President, we became aware of the challenge of getting sisters to attend Homemaking meetings without guilt or bribes. In those glorious days the presidency had a board representative of women throughout our diverse stake. We spent time pondering the concept of Homemaking meeting and the value it had for our sisters. Complaints and excuses were repetitive: I've been there, done that; I don't need any more projects; I have other demands on my time; I'm tired after working all day, etc. Some benefits of such meetings were obvious: sisters gathering in an informal setting to fellowship each other, an opportunity to bring friends to church, serving, learning, and sharing—especially the delicious refreshments. We asked ourselves, "What would be worth time away from home and effort braving seasonal elements to come to church again?"

Dialogue combined with prayer led us to use the Church Handbook Welfare Wheel—Personal and Family Preparedness as the guide for Homemaking Meetings. Sections of the wheel featured Literacy & Education; Career Development; Financial & Resource Management; Home Production & Storage; Physical Health; Social, Emotional & Spiritual Strength. Each Relief Society group could select topics of interest and need. Beneficial skills and information could blend with gospel principles to enrich lives in an encouraging venue.

Perhaps unfairly, Homemaking Meeting carried connotations limited to crafts and cooking, so we felt one additional change was needed—a new name. Again after prayerful consideration, "Enrichment" evening sounded right, inviting, and worthwhile.

Several months later while crossing the country for a visit in Salt Lake City, I had the opportunity to visit with a counselor in the Relief Society General Presidency. I recounted the deliberations of our Stake Relief Society Board and reported our conclusions. Sister T. responded that "Home" was a universal concept reaching across many boundaries for the Church, and that a name change for Homemaking Meeting did not seem likely.

We had a cordial visit, and as I was leaving the building she asked if I had seen the Homemaking display on a lower level. "I think you will find it of interest," she said.

She was right. The display was a visualization encouraging the use of the Welfare Wheel— Personal and Family Preparedness for Relief Society Homemaking Meetings.

Needless to say, I was amazed and in awe to see before my eyes evidence that God hears and answers prayers. The Spirit bears witness across miles and through periods of time. What is perhaps most important is the desire to seek and confirm our Father's will and, striving together as sisters, to build His Kingdom.

While we assemble monthly to "meet critical needs" and provide "service wherever it is needed," there is groundwork that needs to be done. Will I really talk with the women in my ward about these gritty issues if I haven't developed a bond with them? Not likely. How can I develop these connections? Some of it will happen at Sunday meetings and with visiting teaching. But sometimes what I need is downtime with the gals. Time to not have to think hard. Time to enjoy that underappreciated commodity called "small talk" which provides unguarded peeks into our souls, little touch points for deeper connections. An activity can be a foil for something more meaningful under construction. There is still room in this vision of a relevant Relief

Society for glue guns or crochet hooks. I promise I'll send all my potholders to the needy.

You might say, "I'm not creative." I'm here to tell you, you are. You are creators. Have you ever coaxed a smile from a baby? Have you ever taught someone to forgive? Have you helped someone learn to read? Prepared a family home evening? Organized a family reunion? Possibly you were prompted to do something for a person that you visit teach that made a great difference in their lives. If you have done some of these things, you have been creative.

The raw materials of creation are all around us. President David O. McKay taught: "Sculptors of life are we, with our uncarved souls before us. Everyone of us is carving a soul."

—Mary Ellen Smoot

Family Gatherings
A handout prepared by Patty Shelley Bushman

"It is not enough to think family is important. We need to do things to support the family, to be vocal and direct about how important it is."
—Susan Abel Lieberman, *New Traditions*

Every action in this life touches on some chord that will vibrate in eternity.

Eight steps to a Happy Family Gathering

1. Plan, Plan, Plan!
2. Keep everyone informed
3. Involve everyone in activities
4. Have a unifying event daily
5. Provide free time daily
6. Have some surprises
7. Be flexible
8. Don't make it too costly

Activities/Events/Ideas for a Reunion

- Instigate a roll call (produce a tangible family tree)
- Create an ancestor quiz
- Research/publish ancestor histories
- Create/publish family histories
- Provide family T-shirts/hats, matching outfits
- Have a family photo taken
- Create a commemorative poster for the event
- Put on a "show" incorporating a family theme
- Art competition for younger children (prizes for all)
- Provide a craft-making activity with a family twist
- Shoot a video (an original, religious, or family story)
- Choose teams and have athletic competitions
- Provide a take-away gift for the children
- Provide a time for a "testimony" or family meeting

Activities/Events/Ideas for a Wedding Anniversary

- Invite friends and family to a dinner/party
- Have a separate family dinner
- Create a memory book of photos and letters

- Create a friendship quilt
- Have a family photo taken
- Provide family T-shirts
- Research/produce a history of the couple
- Create a family directory
- Produce a family calendar
- Write a musical based on the couple's life

There was audible laughter in the chapel when I was sustained as Enrichment Leader. I didn't mind, though. I was laughing harder than anyone. Even the bishop, when he issued the call, told me, "I know so many people who'd like to witness this." I knew for certain that God has a keen sense of irony.

Forget crafts—I couldn't even tie a decent bow. Forget table cloths and centerpieces—I was only "domestic" if I had to be. I was also teaching an evening class the same night as Enrichment Meeting. I wouldn't even be able to attend for at least four months. But I was determined to be true to myself and fulfill the calling the best I knew how. After all, God knew who He was calling. Right?

I spent several months trying to find my niche, a way to bring my own unique talents to the calling. At first, I was just loaning my body to the cause: hands, feet, mouth, brain. I made phone calls. I tied malformed bows on invitations and delivered food to be cooked for a dinner I couldn't attend. I helped organize and run a half-day November craft day. I had never seen so many glue guns in my life.

But it wasn't until December that I truly felt I had been able to contribute my self to the calling. As we met to plan our December Enrichment Meeting, we noticed it fell on the same week as the ward Christmas party, a weeknight rehearsal for the children's program, and regularly scheduled youth activities. That was in addition to school concerts and performances, holiday shopping and baking—all valid demands on sisters' time.

As we debated how to help the sisters feel the true spirit of the Christmas season, I could only conclude that all of us would be better served by one less obligation. I also knew that canceling a church meeting could be seen as downright heretical. I suggested it anyway. Cancel Enrichment? The sisters on the committee stopped, stunned. Then they giggled. Then they sighed. And elected me to run it past the bishop.

He agreed.

We cancelled.

Or "refocused." We sent each sister home with a letter encouraging her to spend the evening with her family, neighbors, or friends, celebrating the season. We attached a chocolate-covered mint candy stick to stir into hot chocolate, with the saying, "To see the sacred, we must slow down." I don't know how many sisters followed that advice. But at least we had given them the option—all tied up with malformed bows.

A recent, fun Enrichment Meeting was a newlywed/friend game complete with music from the TV show. Friends in the ward were paired up and had to guess how their friend would respond to certain questions. Many of the sisters had not laughed that hard in a long time. That may not be the goal of the General Relief Society presidency, but I think it was what a lot of us needed that night.

Another night we had three different service options: the Leprosy Bandage Project, kits for displaced children, and making curtains for a women's and children's homeless shelter in the city. Women who knew all about these projects shared information. Then those who wanted to sign up for one or all did so. We felt we were getting at the basics of Relief Society, and it felt great.

One of the most beautiful nights was a Christmas event looking at fine art depicting the birth of the Savior. Sisters had prepared interesting presentations on each piece. It was lovely and would have been a fabulous thing to invite a friend to attend.

Years ago in one ward, Sister J., a saintly woman, made 75 large sugared Easter eggs for people to decorate and put a scene of a bunny, etc., inside. We never had so many people attend an event. Sisters came out of the woodwork—active and inactive. It was a great event, even if we did not see many of the "less active" sisters the next day at church.

One year when I was in a ward Relief Society presidency we decided our theme for the year would be "service." Each month we had a different service project. For each of our Enrichment nights, the sisters were asked to bring something in support of the service project, or the evening was spent working on the project itself. Some of our activities throughout the year included:

- ·Gathering toiletries for a local Salvation Army shelter.
- ·A Spring and Fall food drive for an inner-city ward.
- ·A Spring cleaning clothing donation to an inner-city, inter-faith church.
- ·Picking blueberries, making blueberry jam, and distributing jars to sisters who accomplished the Book of Mormon reading challenge.
- ·A school supplies drive for an inner-city ward.
- ·Making baby quilts for a local hospital.
- ·Crocheting and knitting leper bandages which were donated to LDS Humanitarian Services.
- ·Choosing items on an "Angel" Christmas tree and donating presents to under-privileged families.

It was a marvelous year. Our mind-set was to think of what we could do for others and focus less on ourselves. At the beginning of the year we felt it was important to do things both within the church and for our community, and we felt we had achieved our goals.

It all started in December when the Young Women decided to make Christmas stockings for the Primary children of an inner-city ward. As I saw them stuffing the stockings with goodies, I reflected on the food drive we had for this same ward just before Thanksgiving. As I was coordinating the donations and counting all the cans of corn, I was reminded of the importance of food on one's table. At the same time, it occurred to me that even though a can of corn is essential, receiving it doesn't necessarily make you feel special. I suddenly wished we also had a Christmas project for the sisters in this ward to make them feel special, but it was too late . . . or was it?

We had been conservative with our money in Relief Society so we had money left in our budget at the end of the year. After Christmas I proposed my idea to the rest of the presidency, and we all decided to press forward. A sister in our ward donated her collection of large canning jars; I donated the fabric and ribbon; and with our surplus money we bought flour, sugar, and chocolate chips. The next month our Enrichment evening consisted of making Cookie Mix Mason Jars—one for each sister in the inner-city ward. Only their bishop and Relief Society president knew we were coming when we descended the Sunday before Valentine's Day. We brought in box after box of cookie jars—88 to be exact. It was heavenly to see the smiles on those sisters' faces as we passed out their special Valentine's gift. It was just a little thing, but we felt the love in their hearts as we shared our love with them.

❧

What I remember most is Sister S.'s class on home repairs where she showed us a tool that's used for cleaning the coils on refrigerators (the one that looks like a giant mascara wand), and the time I wanted to go to a writing class so badly that I said, "Who cares if my face is so dry it looks like I ought to be featured in a dermatology textbook?" and I went anyway.

In my ward in New England we had a great time throwing birthday luncheons for all the ward Relief Society sisters. We did them at a home and invited all sisters who had birthdays that month. Most people came, including many less active sisters. I loved how it reunited sisters in different ways. The time of the event might have to be adjusted in a ward where many sisters work. This addressed one of the issues that I struggle with in Church callings. As a Relief Society president, it seemed like I spent so much time with the very small percentage of women with problems and so often, that those without problems were sort of ignored. The birthday luncheons were a great way to enjoy time with everyone and the older sisters in the ward really liked them.

When I was Homemaking Counselor, I was blessed with a Homemaking Leader who was willing to be the "nuts and bolts" woman to my "philosophy and tactics" role. We had a great partnership. (I hope she agrees.) I knew that some women moaned and complained about anything craft related.

Others loved that sort of thing. We always tried to have a selection of some handy project for the artsy types; something for intellectual or life skills improvement; and often a cooking or domestics class. We had refreshments at every meeting, of course. Here's a version of the Homemaking/ Enrichment survey we had the ladies fill out at our opening social.

Interest Survey

We want to know what your needs and interests are. Please be candid and, if possible, generous with your interests and enthusiasm. Please also cut the other sisters a little slack for finding some things interesting that you may find truly dumb or boring.

In general I think crafts are:

1. Tacky and pointless.
2. Sometimes fun, but I'm picky.
3. Intimidating. I'm a klutz but would secretly like to try something.
4. Fun once in a while.
5. One of my favorite pastimes. I really like this category!
6. Other _____

Relative to crafts I consider myself:

1. A novice.
2. A wanna-be.
3. Experienced.
4. Phobic.
5. An enemy.

If you are not an enemy of crafts please list the kinds of craft courses you'd enjoy . . .

(Note: on our survey we listed a number of options for classes in each category as well as allowing space for the sisters to write in their own suggestions.)

In general I think cooking is:

1. Tacky and pointless.
2. Sometimes fun, but I'm picky.
3. Intimidating. I'm a klutz but would secretly like to try something.
4. Fun once in a while.
5. One of my favorite pastimes. I really like this category!
6. Other _____

Relative to cooking I consider myself:

1. A novice.
2. A wanna-be.
3. Experienced.
4. Phobic.
5. An enemy.

If you are not an enemy of cooking, please list the kinds of cooking courses you'd enjoy . . .

In general I think intellectual enrichment is:
1. Tacky and pointless.
2. Sometimes fun, but I'm picky.
3. Intimidating. I'm a klutz but would secretly like to try something.
4. Fun once in a while.

5. One of my favorite pastimes. I really like this category!
6. Other _____

If you answered anything other than #1, please list the kinds of intellectual enrichment you enjoy . . .

I would be willing to teach a class on:
1. Something someone else suggests.
2. Something I already know how to do such as

_____

3. Something specific, but give me some time to think about what I'd like to do.

Other ideas are welcome! Please call the Enrichment Leader at . . .

A few last items. Circle or complete the ones that apply to you.
1. I will occasionally need childcare.
2. I'm not likely to attend Enrichment because . . .

_____

3. Please, never ask me to teach anything. Just let me come and enjoy myself.
4. Please, never ask me to bring or make refreshments.
5. I would be interested in a longer, separate gathering with women who want to do a particular project, learn a special skill, or go on a field trip to a special place. Please specify.

❧

I have never been on an Enrichment committee, but I have ideas as to what I would do. My experience is that it is always harder to do one class than to do a series. Besides, I find it too superficial and frustrating to have 20 minute introductions to yoga, LDS art, the 72-hour-kit, and other useful and complex matters. So what I would do is to run three six-session participatory miniclasses at a time, beginning a new one every three months. These would depend on the makeup of the unit and the desires of the sisters, but some I would value are:

- Music in the Church.
- Grandmother ideas and resources.
- Historical lessons such as a series on the early Relief Society, individual classes on the presidents, women in the church, church history in our local areas.
- An ongoing course on journal or other writing and family history.
- Personal presentations where we tell of our lives.
- A "sit and sew" class where people bring their mending or handwork or tie quilts.

In the church, the people and the process are always more valuable than the product. The major purpose of these classes should be to build the relationships of sisterhood. We do that best when we work together on projects and committees. Participating is what makes Enrichment valuable.

❧

The Homemaking leader and I brainstormed on topics and came up with what we thought of as an appealing assortment. Coming up with clever titles for our activities sometimes made a big difference. It was very satisfying to have sisters complain that they didn't like having to choose among such good options. Some of the topics sounded dull to me, but by selecting a dynamic teacher even the driest topics came to life.

Here are some of the miniclasses we suggested or actually presented. Feel free to use them or adapt them to your situation. Many of these may be distinctly inappropriate for your setting; others might be close but need adapting. In many cases these require getting a teacher who is already familiar with the topic or who is willing to do some thorough research beforehand.

Some of these may seem far afield from the current emphasis on relevance ("juggling and other attention getting stunts" for example) but there may be method to the madness. Investigator families, neighbors, classmates, and colleagues may be drawn to the Latter-day Saint who knows how to juggle, solve a Rubik's cube, or pull a quarter out of someone's ear!

Be prayerful and creative in tying them to the spiritual topic presented at the beginning of the night. Some suggested class topics include:

Kitchen, Foods & Meals

- All you ever wanted to know about cranberries (or other food common to your area)
- Soups & Chowders
- Vietnamese egg rolls
- New England Cooking
- Elegant Brunches
- Nutrition basics
- Using your Noodle: Pasta and Sauces
- Low Fat Cooking
- Picnic and Travel Food
- Ways with Herbs in oils and vinegars
- Shortcakes and cobblers
- Bread basics
- Specialty breads and pastry
- Cold cuts and sandwiches
- Carbs, schmarbs—A look at diet styles
- Punch and cookie favorites
- Jams & preserves
- Lettuce entertain you: salads for all
- Can you can?
- Food storage basics
- International favorite foods
- Use and abuse of chopsticks
- Living by microwave alone
- Diets for Diabetics
- Basics of cleaning fish
- Terrific Tofu
- Exactly what does a convection oven do?
- Meals for missionaries to make
- Cooking for crowds
- Potatoes: from "funeral" to "festive"

·What do all these utensils do?
·Cookies: from simple to labor intensive

Visual Arts & Crafts

·Iron-on Halloween Wall Hanging
·Eucalyptus wreaths
·Basic Crocheting & Knitting
·Basic Oil Painting
·Rubber Stamp Basics
·Accordion books
·Making a canvas teepee for kids
·Collage and mosaic
·Tin Punch Ornaments
·Creating apple head dolls
·Ukranian egg decorating
·Plastic egg / Easter scripture sets for kids
·Sidewalk chalk arts, crafts & games
·You old sew-n-sew! Needle and thread basics
·Handmade soaps
·Campfire fun and games
·Making quiet books & flannel boards
·Finger Plays for Tiny Tots
·Orchids and other fussy flowers
·Getting plants to grow
·Hair braiding and Summer Hair-do's
·Salsa dance and music
·Hula lessons and island crafts
·Introduction to leading music
·How to play the harmonica
·Juggling and other attention getting stunts
·Holidays around the globe
·Fabrics around the world

·Batik techniques
·Quilting—history and practice

Fine Arts

·The Spiritual Lives of the Composers
·Ballet seminar
·Shakespearean Lingo, Thou wench!
·Famous women authors
·Classical music for dummies
·A sisters poetry slam
·Haiku workshop
·The art of the personal essay
·10,000 commonly misspelled words
·Fairy tales through the ages
·LDS artists, poets & authors
·What makes an orchestra?
·Hands-on instrument demonstrations
·Up and comers in the music world
·Folk music traditions

Of Local Interest

·Local nature trails and habitats
·Sightseeing in the area
·Making the most of the local library
·Biographies of town founders
·Bargain shopping in the area
·Antiquing in our area
·Cultural diversity awareness
·Other faith traditions in our area
·Navigating the neighborhoods: getting to know
  the public transportation system
·Service opportunities in our community

·Touring the local museums
·Touring the town cemetery
·Recycling in our area
·Our area's famous and infamous folks
·How's and who's of our local government
·Hungry and homeless in our area

Healthcare

·Fundamentals of prenatal care
·Women's Health Issues/ Breast Cancer
·Creating First Aid kits
·Poisons and antidotes
·Dealing with Alzheimer's
·Tricks to keeping mentally sharp
·CPR and First Aid workshop
·Self defense for women
·Rape prevention and crisis help
·Foot health
·Taking time to breathe
·Veterinary medicine basics for the pets we love
·Child abuse prevention
·Prostate & testicular cancer
·Dealing with our own or someone else's chronic
  illness
·OB/GYN issues and sexuality
·Fertility and Infertility
·Deaf in a hearing world
·Special Needs & Spirituality
·Eating Disorders

High Tech
·Introduction to the Internet

- Bargain shopping on the Internet
- eBay can be your friend
- Basics of digital photography
- What you can do with a video camera
- Cells phones and what they can do
- Scripture study in our modern age
- Off the grid—what does that mean?
- All the latest gizmos
- Home security systems

Social & Emotional Well-Being

- When someone you love is grieving: what helps and what hurts
- He said; she said: How men and women communicate differently
- 12 step programs
- Understanding the welfare system
- Help! I've got teenagers!
- Healing after a broken marriage
- Child abuse prevention
- What Church social services can do
- Understanding the welfare system
- Teaching healthy sexuality & modesty
- When your eternal family is dysfunctional
- Dealing with our own or someone else's chronic illness
- Eating disorders
- Making amends; learning forgiveness
- Hungry and homeless in our area
- What I wish I'd known before I got married, had children, grew old, etc.
- Being single in a "married" church

·Pampering yourself
·Learning to be still
·Finding peace in a turbulent world
·Assertiveness training
·Being willing to accept help
·Anxiety disorders & depression
·Therapy: which kinds do what?
·Fertility and Infertility

LDS Interests and Family History

·Introduction to family history research
·Planning Family Reunions
·Surviving Family Night
·Creating an ancestor quiz
·Conserving documents and history
·Highlights of the Pioneer Trek
·Public speaking tips and troubles
·Missions for seniors
·Women in the scriptures
·Scripture study in our modern age
·Stories behind the hymns
·Exploring the Seder and Passover
·Sharing Sister missionary experiences
·Spirituality and special needs
·Women in LDS history
·Sharing our favorite scriptures
·The growth of the church in Africa
·The gospel around the globe: what's the same
  and what's different

Basic Domestics & Life /Job Skills

·Basic auto repair

·Closet organizing do's and don'ts
·Out, out, darn spot! Stains and how to elimi-
    nate them
·Housekeeping essentials: who can do what?
·Tools and what they do
·Top ten most neglected maintenance chores
    that will save you $$$
·Wardrobe essentials for our climate
·Crime and fire prevention at home
·Navigating the neighborhoods: getting to know
    the public transportation system
·Travel tips for planes, trains, and automobiles
·The savvy shopper: getting more for your
    money
·Electronics workshop
·Plumbing essentials
·Job hunting skills & networking
·Financial management & planning
·Wills & Estate Planning
·What kinds of insurance to you need?
·Investing your nest egg
·Tax issues for women
·Resume writing
·Is online banking for you?
·Learning to lead; being willing to follow

History, Social Studies & Popular Culture

·Women in the Colonial Era
·Conserving documents and history
·Native American history and culture in our
    area
·How dark were the Dark Ages?

·Women during WWII
·History of the Middle East
·Life in Moscow
·Experiences in South Africa
·The European Union
·U.S. National Parks
·Diplomacy at home and abroad
·ABC's of the FBI, CIA & Homeland Security
·Crime & punishment: our legal system
·Deaf in a hearing world
·Couch potatoes unite: good things on TV
·Panel on the pros and cons of censorship
·Child labor laws
·History of women's right to vote
·Preparing for an empty nest
·Education issues for women
·"Family" through history

I attended a "Ballet for Dummies" class that was fascinating. The teacher spoke of the history of ballet, which has changed quite drastically over the centuries. She discussed differences in style of dancing and costumes between various areas of the world. She showed several video clips to emphasize and illustrate the information. It was especially fascinating to see a ballerina perform both before and after becoming anorexic. There was obvious decline in her energy and ability to gain height in jumps. The desire for an extremely thin look is a modern aspect of modern ballet.

The Spirit bears witness across miles and through periods of time. What is perhaps most important is the desire to seek and confirm our Father's will and, striving together as sisters, to build His Kingdom.

Diane Alumway

One Enrichment Night a nurse spoke to us about women's health issues. She brought with her useful pamphlets about menstruation, menopause, breast cancer, diet requirements, and even a prosthetic breast with lumps in it for us all to feel, detect and count. We had a very meaningful discussion that was of interest to women of all ages. (Not just those of us who were noticeably aging!)

Years ago one of my most cherished sisters required a mastectomy. When she went for her first chemotherapy session, no one had prepared her for the lengthy process of intravenous drip that caused a metallic taste in her mouth. All she could do was sit and think of the disease that was ravaging her body and this poison that was being put into her veins.

She came up with the idea of creating activity bags for the hospital to give to women undergoing chemotherapy. We sewed the bags and enclosed a women's magazine, a few note cards and a pen, a stick of chewing gum and a few hard candies to counter the awful taste, simple cross stitch instructions and the materials to complete the project, a crossword puzzle and maybe one or two other items to pass the time. I remember the activity vividly because I knew and loved this woman so much. Because I mourned with her and tried in small ways to bear her burdens, I was able to imagine all those other women as individuals, needing to occupy their time and their minds.

The Relief Society president I later served with said that the service projects were always the most engaging for the sisters. She knew that the feedback would be universally positive. My guess is that with the advanced state of telecommunications, we see and hear the needs of individuals many times a day. When we recognize our connectedness to so many, we could feel powerless and overwhelmed. Instead, actively doing almost anything to help creates just the opposite experience. We are empowered and acknowledge the hope for all of us.

Sister R. works at Children's Hospital in our town on the floor where they do lumbar punctures and spinal taps. In order to do these procedures, the child must curl over a pillow to allow access to the spine. Sister R. found that the regular sized pillows were too large for the toddlers and younger children to curl over easily so she designed a smaller pillow to accommodate their size.

Sister R. approached the sisters in her ward, and they began making the pillows for a service project. At our Home, Family, and Personal Enrichment training this past fall, the stake presidency asked if all the wards in our stake would make these "procedure pillows." We were each given a pillow with a pillowcase, the necessary measurements, and sent on our way.

At our January Enrichment meeting we held a "Pillow Fight." We even wore our pajamas. Sisters in the ward provided all the supplies to make the pillows and cases. To begin the evening we had a short lesson on service and then the fight began. We divided the cultural hall up into four team areas, each supplied with a cutting table, stuffing table, and sewing table equipped with a regular sewing machine, a serger, and an example pillow and case. The sisters divided into random teams and had thirty minutes to complete as many procedure pillows with cases as possible. The winners received Hershey bars.

After the official contest was over, the sisters kept sewing until it was time to leave. Through the course of the evening we made 60 pillows with cases with 16 more in various stages of completion. Our donated total was 76! The evening was wonderfully loud with conversation, friendly competition, the spirit of service, and most of all love for the children. It was an amazing activity that prepared and ran itself. Our sisters left excited and happy. We had done service together, lifted our spirits together, and become closer sisters.

Sister R. was delighted and said she thought our pillows would be about a three month supply. The hospital is now using these pillows to provide comfort to other children in the hospital, too, to provide them with something familiar to have with them no matter what they are going through.

Procedure Pillow instructions:

Materials:
> Cotton/cotton blend fabrics—must be new (do not wash fabric)
> Thread
> Poly filling—new (a 20 oz. bag fills approximately 2 pillows)
> Serger/ sewing machine (if using a sewing machine, use 1/4" seams)

Pillow (13" x 17" finished dimensions)
1. Cut fabric 13" x 34".
2. Fold in half and serge or sew long sides.
3. Turn right side out and stuff.
4. Serge or sew open end closed.

Pillow Case (14" x 20" finished dimensions)
1. Cut fabric 14" x 42".
2. Fold in half and serge or sew long sides.
3. Turn right side out and fold unfinished edge in 1".
4. Fold in edge 1" again and stitch close to edge.

Around Valentine's Day we were invited to make Valentine's cards for Enrichment Night. I looked forward to this Enrichment activity like I hadn't many others—relishing the chance to make cards for friends and family, with my children unable to attack my work, and supplies generously donated by the ward. When I arrived, however, I must admit I felt let down. Instead of the crafting free-for-all I'd planned on, we were to draw two names of women in our ward and make Valentine's cards for them from carefully prepared kits, making me feel less creative by the minute. I drew two names and went to sit in the back.

As I painstakingly applied glue from a toothpick onto the backs of small flowers and then applied the small flowers to the card in the shape of a stenciled heart, I began to regret having come. Not only would these two cards take up my entire time at Enrichment, now I had the added assignment of writing something kind in them and delivering them with a small gift to two sisters.

Later that night, however, as I wrote on those cards, I was able to express to sisters who I did not know well some of the good things I noticed about them from a distance. When I got my handmade card from a sister who I didn't know well (along with a quart of orange juice for my kids), it made such a difference to me that I have since tried to be more conscientious about expressing my sometimes silent compliments.

For Valentine's Day one year we had a lesson on strengthening the ties of marriage. (This may not work in all wards, but in mine we have very few single sisters, so it seemed OK to do one lesson that was specifically geared to the married set.) All of the sisters took a "Five Love Languages" test someone had found online. We talked about how we scored.

It was very interesting to see how we expressed and received love so differently from one another. Each sister also took a copy of the test home for her husband. After talking about our tests, we all made special Valentine's Day gift bags for our husbands, with candy and cut-out slips of paper. Each piece of paper had a suggested "special something" on it, such as getting tickets to a concert or offering to give your spouse a night on the town. Each week my husband and I now draw from our gift bag and post our slips on the refrigerator to remind ourselves to do that special thing for each other.

One Enrichment Night we gathered in the backyard of one of the sisters, and three women shared some of their favorite books. Though they hadn't been assigned categories, one shared children's books, another novels, and the last focused on Church books. Their short presentations led to wonderful discussions about other good books, and we took notes on new book ideas. I still have my list of books from that evening and I've already read almost one-third of the books.

A favorite Enrichment Night was a Christmas/December night we did years ago. The Relief Society presidency (of which I was a member) had saved our budget all year long so that the sisters would not have to bring any of the refreshments. We actually had it catered—amazing, yummy desserts straight from a fancy baker! And we asked the sisters to bring a gift for themselves. That's right—not for charity, or for someone more needy, but a gift they really wanted, but that no one would probably give to them. Each sister then shared with everyone what she was giving herself that year, and why. Some of the "gifts" included a shower curtain, a portrait of one sister's daughter, a book, a new music CD, and a new hairstyle! It was so lovely to see these sisters actually think about themselves for just a day, and to share in food they didn't have to make!

One woman in our ward is a professional caterer, and she treated the sisters to a wonderful sit-down dinner to celebrate the Relief Society's birthday. Many times, our church meals are paper-plate-in-the-lap affairs, but this was a full-blown event with china and all. I wasn't able to go and I still regret it! Everyone loved being pampered like that.

At Christmas we had a progressive dinner party which was a huge hit. We started with appetizers in one house, a main course in another, and dessert in a third. In our spread-out ward this was a bit challenging, and the "meeting" lasted over three hours because of all the driving. In places where church members live close together I think that this kind of thing would be ideal. At each house we had a short lesson on holiday traditions somewhere in the world: a quick introduction to Hanukkah complete with a lighted menorah; a little talk on Christmas in Poland by the mother of a missionary there; a lovely history of Christmas in Germany by a sister who used to live there. The snacks were related to the nations and traditions we learned about.

One cold January night, we had a "chicken soup" evening where we all brought a sweet or funny story to share with the group. There were some real tear-jerker moments. One especially memorable part of the night was learning that one of our new converts was something of a poet; she read aloud some of the poetry she had written for her children. I don't know if we ever would have learned that about her otherwise, as she is quite shy. And of course, we finished out the evening with a delicious round of homemade chicken noodle soups and breads.

In our ward we have a growing number of Hispanic converts, and one of the most helpful Enrichment meetings I've ever been to was one where the missionaries came and described some of the challenges that immigrants in our area face. One Mexican-born convert came to Enrichment and the missionaries translated for everyone, so that she could answer our questions and tell us her story. It was so marvelous to be able to get to know her a little better, and that meeting prompted our ward to start a Spanish class so that members have even borne their testimonies in halting, beautiful Spanish during fast and testimony meeting.

We had a fine and well-attended service project where we created care packages for U.S. troops serving in Iraq. Not all of the sisters agree about the morality of the war, but we found we could unite in meeting the needs of the troops. It provided some unity in a divisive time.

Our ward had a project under the auspices of the Stake Public Affairs Committee. They purchased children's books, tape recorded them at an Enrichment Night activity and then one of the members of our ward flew to Afghanistan to deliver them. As a follow up at another Enrichment Night, the man who delivered the tapes and books spoke to the group. He had spent two weeks in Afghanistan. Most of the time was spent going through special committees who had to listen to the tapes to make sure no subversive material was being passed through to the children. He then found three different orphanages where he was able to make the donations. Hundreds of stories and tapes were delivered during his visit. The stake is now working on enlarging the project and sending more tapes to the country.

The women who taped the books have fond memories about how they picked their favorite book, wrote a note, sometimes sent a picture, and then taped recorded the story. It felt like a true service to a very needy group, and they felt they were making a little dent in the misery over there.

The man who made the delivery has traveled throughout the world but felt that experience of finding "homes" for these books/tapes was one of his most fulfilling trips. Anyone interested in knowing more can check out the website:

www.voicestoafghanistan.org.

We had a great lesson on stress relief with a professional massage therapist on hand to teach us how to give massages. The sisters enjoyed taking turns as the therapist's guinea pig, and trying their new techniques out on each other.

When I get home from teaching first grade all day I am bone-tired and find it difficult to go to Enrichment Meeting. But I have found over the years that when I do go, even for just a little while, I learn at least one new thing that changes my life.

One of those times involved a plant project I had been teaching my first graders for years: Hairy Harrys. The children decorated a plastic cup with a face, filled the cup with dirt, and topped it with soaked wheat. When the wheat grew it looked like hair. To get the wheat to sprout I first had to empty one of my cupboards at school in order to have a dark place to put the cups. Then I covered all the cups with a wet dish towel that had to be checked every few hours, even on weekends, to make sure it stayed wet. Over the years the dampness of the cups and cloth warped the wooden shelf in the cupboard. The project was as complicated as it was messy.

One Tuesday night, too tired to go to the entire meeting, I slipped in the Relief Society room about halfway through Enrichment. One of the sisters was just starting her demonstration on how to make "real" Easter grass using soaked wheat. Instead of putting it on dirt, she showed how you can put the wheat on top of Vermiculite and place it on a window sill.

My mouth dropped open. This was my Hairy Harrys idea made a thousand times easier. Now that plant project is simple, clean, easy, and fun. Every year as we study plants I appreciate how ten minutes at Enrichment changed my life.

All of our sisters need stronger ties with one another in an environment that bolsters faith and strengthens families and supports struggles. Creating such a place with such opportunities is the work of Relief Society.
—Bonnie D. Parkin

❧

The first time I was called to serve on a Homemaking committee, I was a new freshman at BYU. My only previous experience with the Relief Society Homemaking program was watching my mother and the other women in our ward knit afghans to be sold at the annual bazaar, teach each other how to quilt, and figure out what to do with the hundreds of pounds of wheat they had stored in their garages. In other words, to me, "homemaking" meant "making stuff for the home." Such a concept presented challenges for a novice leader whose entire Relief Society lived in 10' x 14' dorm rooms. I presented lessons on decorating bulletin boards and cooking tasty snacks in a popcorn popper, and we had fun—but I doubt that I helped anyone prepare to strengthen their future families or learn to apply gospel principles in their lives.

Some years later, while my husband and I were in graduate school, I was again asked to serve on a Homemaking committee with a unique set of challenges. The inner-city branch we attended was dominated by university students and faculty members; but it was 1979, only a year after President Kimball received the revelation that broke down race-based barriers to the blessings of the priesthood. The largely African-American community in which we lived was beginning to respond to our increased missionary efforts. Many of the women who found hope in the restored gospel and joined our branch arrived with little education and few practical skills. Following the counsel of the

Relief Society presidency, our Homemaking committee instituted a "Back to Basics" program to teach the fundamentals: first aid, sanitation, childcare, cooking, and sewing.

The most avid participant in the sewing class I taught was a good-natured woman named Sadie. She lived in a cramped apartment in a blighted area of town, but she was one of the fortunate few who had a dependable husband as well as a passel of children. Both Sadie and Vincent worked hard, determined to provide their family with a better life than the one most of their neighbors had settled for. They were grateful for whatever help their new church family had to offer.

I helped Sadie choose an easy pattern for her first sewing project—a skirt. The fabric she had brought to work on was as bright as her smile, and her enthusiasm infused the whole class. No one was prouder of her finished product than Sadie— even though the skirt's seams puckered a little and the fit was kind of snug across the hips. And no one was prouder than I to have taught Sadie a useful homemaking skill.

With graduate school behind us, my husband and I moved on. Sadie moved away from the city, too, when Vincent was offered a good job in another state. About ten years later, I ran into Sadie again at a women's conference. This time she was the teacher, presenting a talk on developing leadership skills. Obviously, she and Vincent and their family had prospered, thanks to hard work and determination.

Over lunch at the conference, Sadie and I reminisced about our days in the inner-city branch, and I mentioned the sewing class.

"That skirt!" she laughed. "First and last thing I ever made!"

I tried not to let my face fall in disappointment. I guess I wanted to hear her say that learning to sew had changed her life, had made it possible for her to save enough money to send a child to college or something. But as I listened to more of her story, I realized that there was no reason to feel disappointed. Sadie may not have embraced sewing, but she embraced the gospel and the community of Saints. My Homemaking Meeting class—and dozens that followed—helped her to feel at home in Relief Society and in the church. Those enrichment opportunities helped her recognize her own unique talents, and the leadership skills she developed as she learned to serve as well as to sew have been a blessing to her, her family, and her community.

Wendy and Tom moved into our ward with their three children. They were a model LDS family with strong testimonies of the gospel. Because Tom had an excellent job with lots of foreign travel, a high salary and many wonderful experiences, some people in our ward felt intimidated and envious. Another contributing cause was the fact that Wendy wore the hugest diamond ring any of us had ever seen, the sort of ring that came through the door before she did.

In one memorable Enrichment Night we heard the story behind it. Both Wendy and Tom had come from poor families. Wendy's father had been an alcoholic. Tom was from a largely uneducated family and his early schooling had been sporadic. They met at college and married shortly afterwards. It was the story of their wedding that Wendy related in a "Share Your Worst Experience" Enrichment Night that endeared us to Wendy forever.

In hilarious terms she described how her mother insisted that her own best friend make Wendy's wedding dress. A pattern was chosen that, had it been made from the soft silk in the fabric indications, would have been flattering and elegant. Instead it turned out, in the "bullet-proof" polyester chosen for its cheapness by Mother's friend, to be hideous and bulky. The fashionable bow at her neck became a throat-slicing, chin-chafing hindrance. She also had a hair disaster when the dye solution reacted unfavorably with her voluminous hair, and it began to fall out in great clumps.

As it turned out the dress and hair became almost entirely invisible when Tom turned up in the loudest possible checked suit topped by his new pride and joy—an immense moustache. It certainly didn't help any when during the exchanging of the vows in the actual wedding ceremony, the officiator loudly chided them with, "Say it like you mean it!"

Wendy had big dreams for a beautiful and elegant wedding reception, but her parents were having none of it. "What's good enough for us is good enough for you, young lady," they would say. The cultural hall, barely disguised, was what she got, plus a punch made of Kool-Aid with unprecedented amounts of sugar. We've all seen beautiful weddings in cultural halls and how lucky we are to have them; however, Wendy could scarcely hold back the tears when she saw how the strobe light just about finished off any hope of romantic mystique. Through the blur she could certainly no longer perceive the almost invisible pin-prick of the tiny diamond on her left hand.

No one could have been more friendly or loving than Wendy who served as our Enrichment Counselor. Her husband wanted to show his gratitude for Wendy's tremendous support and dedication to him while he built his fortune by giving her the most beautiful diamond he could afford. But she said whenever she looked down at it, "I think of what there used to be; I could never forget that."

Thank goodness for Enrichment Night which brings us together as friends and sisters and helps us to stop being judgmental.

I welcomed the opportunity to do an Enrichment Night session on the influence of women in our homes and communities. One of my favorite subjects! So I carefully pulled together material I'd collected over the years. As the capper, I was going to use excerpts from two movies, "The Sound of Music" and "Mary Poppins." I rented the tapes and fast-forwarded them to the scenes I wanted. From "The Sound of Music" I planned to use the part where Captain Von Trapp calls his children by means of a whistle and Maria declares she will not use this harsh means to assemble the family. Then I would use the scene where she calms the children during a thunder storm by singing to them. And a third where Maria dresses them all alike and takes them out for a day of just plain, simple fun. From "Mary Poppins" I wanted to show the rigidness of the Banks household and how Mary gentles them all. I would wind up with Mary singing "Just a spoonful of sugar makes the medicine go down . . ." Feminine influence at its best! The women were showing the men how to do things!

On the evening of the presentation I set up the TV and the VCR. I checked them and everything worked fine. The evening progressed beautifully, beginning with a light supper, expertly done by the magnificent cooks on our Enrichment committee. My presentation went well, with the women laughing in all the right places and nodding their heads at the points I was making. Then it was time for the tapes. I hit the power button. The screen glowed cheerfully. I pressed "play." Nothing happened. I pressed it again. More happy glowing. I tried to stay calm.

Sister A. was a graduate engineer. Surely she could figure out what was wrong. She checked the equipment, adjusted buttons, and did everything but kick the TV. Nothing. Well, Sister K. was getting her doctorate at Caltech. Surely those credentials would convince the VCR to cooperate. They didn't. Maria and Mary had gone off to new adventures and weren't making any appearances that night. Not, at least, during my presentation.

I limped through a sketchy oral wrap-up and drooped to a chair, totally deflated. Later, after the closing prayer, Brother P., our ward electronics genius, came in. I told him what happened. He approached the TV-VCR set-up and touched a couple buttons. Suddenly Maria and Mary returned from wherever they'd been. I laughed as I thanked Brother P. and I realized that those recalcitrant machines had taught me something. Both men and women have excellent qualities to contribute to our homes and communities. Both need to be rescued sometimes. And both can still learn something from the other. Even Captain Von Trapp and Mr. Banks turn out to have their good points after all!

I love to be obedient, eat food from sisters' recipes, and win prizes for my food storage. But I don't love making quilts, though my one experience was enriching.

Back in northeastern Illinois in the early 1960s, our tiny branch was told that missionaries were working to restore Nauvoo. Quilts would be appreciated. We had just four sisters and only one of us had ever quilted, but we honored the call with a "yes."

Perhaps it was I who assumed the quilt was to be used by poor missionaries like ours, struggling to exist in cold and windy Illinois. Our male missionaries offered to help, though they'd never even sewn up a rip, let alone a quilt.

I was a doer. "We'll need material," I stated, and though my bank statement at the end of the month was in cents, not dollars, I bought the material. Cheap but good material, in bright pink and shocking turquoise. One young sister offered her husband Irv's service to design blocks, so they'd be acceptable in this historic place.

"Well," said Irv, as he sketched a beehive, "this could go on one block." We all nodded. "And it should tell a little of the history of the Church which ended up in Utah." (His folks did, but for the rest of us converts, this wasn't the case. But we were supportive.) He drew a picture of a giant saguaro cactus. We nodded, cut the blocks into squares, carbon copied his designs onto the blocks, and embroidered the best we could.

We were pleased with our hard work. We'd all learned to embroider. How enriching! I sewed the blocks together by machine. We had a clean, used blanket, which we situated between front and back and I sewed it all together. Then we were ready for our quilter to teach us how to make tiny stitches and quilt our creation. "Do not tie knots on the surface of the quilt!" she said. So I didn't.

We were almost finished when one of the missionaries tried to shift positions after many long hours of sewing and got the toe of his shoe caught on a long thread. He crawled under the quilt and howled, "Who's not knotting their thread?"

"We're not supposed to," I said, defending my actions.

The missionaries flipped over the quilt and for an hour tied the knots I should have tied.

At last it was finished. I got a box the right size, packed the quilt in it, then put in a warm note: "To help missionaries keep out the cold." My husband sealed it at the shipping area of the factory where he worked and it was on its way. The president of the factory was a good Catholic and sanctioned charitable acts done by these quaint Mormons.

We received a lovely little thank you, and we all felt enriched.

We never knew who got our handiwork . . . until I made a trip to Nauvoo in 2001 and stopped at the social hall to catch a play. No play that night, but the good sister missionary there asked, "Would you like to look around?" We nodded.

After seeing all on the first floor we were ushered upstairs. "You might like to see our collection of historic quilts," she said.

They were eye-boggling works of art! Who ever knew that such craftsmanship and good taste existed way back then among pioneers? Why, back in the thirties when I was a child in the backwoods of Missouri, I slept under denim quilts, the pieces being cut from the back side of legs of overalls which were worn out at the knees. Our guide told us where each quilt had come from. No words could express our awe.

Then, as we were about to leave, there near the stairs was a work of art very familiar—done in bright pink and shocking turquoise.

"And where did this one come from?" I asked.

"Well, we're not sure. No one seems to know. But it is obviously valued."

Of course we told her.

I was enlightened as well. We'd made wrong assumptions thinking we were helping the needy. Instead of donating historical heirlooms, we—the poor ourselves—had set out to warm the body and cheer the soul with bright colors. And what we had to give was found acceptable!

It does not take much living to find out that life almost never turns out the way you planned it. Adversity and affliction come to everyone. Do you know anyone who would not like to change something about themselves or their circumstances? And yet I am sure you know many who go forward with faith. You are drawn to those people, inspired by them, and even strengthened by their examples.

—Mary Ellen Smoot

"Often foster children have to leave their homes abruptly, with their belongings in garbage bags. I want them to have an afghan, something special made just for them, so they know that someone cares." I looked with amazement at this petite 14-year-old young woman who spoke at our Enrichment meeting. Erin decided to undertake this ambitious 4H project a year ago.

She had originally planned to work on the project for a year and set a goal to collect 400. The year was up, she had well over 1,000 afghans, and she wasn't about to quit. "My goal is to collect an afghan for every foster child in the state." (Our state had 10,000!)

Erin made several afghans herself, but she had many others working, too. Having delivered this appeal many times, she had women all over the state crocheting for foster children—women in churches of many faiths, women in nursing homes, women in prison. Some women made 6" squares, some volunteered to sew the squares together, some made entire afghans, some donated yarn or money, some found afghans at garage sales and cleaned them. Some taught other women how to crochet or knit. The afghans ranged in size from tiny (for infants) to large (for strapping teenagers).

Stitched to each finished afghan was a panel with the name of the foster child, surrounded by yarn hearts. Placed in gift bags decorated by elementary school children, the afghans were given to the Department of Social Services for anonymous delivery.

As I listened to this young woman speak, I blinked back tears. It was not only her youthful, selfless sincerity. It was remembering my own son as he went into foster care at age 16. His troubled childhood and adolescence had reached a point where we were no longer able to manage him in our struggling family system. It wasn't until years later that he told me how terribly destructive that foster home had been, although it seemed perfect from the outside. Now, years later, as we're all still trying to heal, my son's contact with me is sporadic. He knows I'm here, and I try not to insert myself into his life too often when I miss him.

That night, others in Relief Society started crocheting afghans for toddlers or young children—easier and quicker to make. But I started crocheting an afghan for a teenager. Squares of brown, tan, cream, stitched together and bordered in rich chocolate brown—with a kaleidoscope of feelings in every stitch.

I didn't have any way to be in touch with my son at that time. Making the afghan was a way of connecting with that 16-year-old boy who went into foster care, whom I couldn't help as much as I wanted then, and whom I can't help as much as I want today. At first I thought I'd ask Erin to see that my afghan went to a teenager by his same name. But then I decided that DSS knows better than I. If a Joshua or an Enrique need it more, I wanted him to have it—to know that somebody cares about him.

As a young mother, Homemaking Meeting was a chance to get out of the house, away from the grind of spilled milk and scattered toys. So it made sense to go even after the worst month of my life.

It should have been a happy time, because my second son, Ethan, was just born. But within minutes of birth, nurses in sterile scrubs rushed him to the intensive care unit, as meningitis took hold in his tiny body. As the weeks dragged by, he remained on a ventilator, unable to breathe on his own. The doctors warned us that, if he lived, the damage would be significant. He would be mentally impaired, as well as physically. They also thought he would be blind.

Shortly after he came home—a month later—Homemaking Night came. I was eager to go. I welcomed the break, but I also hoped to thank the women of the ward for the tremendous service they'd given while Ethan was hospitalized.

And I wanted to show off my new baby. No one in the ward had seen him yet, so this would be his first "public appearance." In truth, he didn't look so good. He'd been born with thick, dark hair, but the nurses had shaved patches of it to make room for intravenous needles. Yellow-green bruises covered his skin and the seizure medication he was on made him bloated and puffy. He had to be attached to an apnea monitor when he slept, so ever-present wires and electrodes sprouted from his sleepers like weeds in a rose garden. But he was my son. To me he looked exquisite.

Ward members had heard about Ethan for weeks while they'd delivered meals and cards, offered prayers and well wishes. I wanted to show them what the fuss was about. So I wrapped the baby up in a blanket and went to Homemaking Meeting.

We all gathered in the Relief Society room as usual. I was a few minutes late and slid into the back row. The Relief Society president was introducing visitors and announcing miniclasses. Then she said, "We have a new member of the ward with us tonight. Lisa, could you introduce him?"

My heart swelled as I stood up and showed off my baby.

"This is Ethan Patrick Turner," I said in a shaky voice as my unpredictable emotions tangled together. Fear of the future mingled with a certain weariness from too many long, anxious nights. I wasn't sure, even as the words came out, how the women would respond.

I didn't have to wait long to find out. Within seconds, the room thundered with spontaneous applause. Everyone in the room clapped. Not polite clapping, but cheering. It was like the women were at a football game instead of Homemaking Meeting. I looked around me and saw tear-filled eyes and glowing faces. Those faces showed that we shared more than miniclasses and home management lessons.

By the way, my son grew from a sick baby into a handsome young man with broad shoulders and a disarming smile. He has been blessed with a strong body and mind. He plays a mean jazz saxophone and is equally skilled as a bassoon player. He will graduate from high school next year and plans to study music in college. The women of my ward were right. He has earned their applause, and more.

Despite serving as Homemaking Leader for years and attending hundreds of these weeknight productions, I don't remember many things from Homemaking/Enrichment night lessons or classes. I do, however, poignantly recall the Wednesday night that I first brought my newborn daughter along. In a way completely different than the Sunday she was held by her father before a congregation, we received—this baby and I—the blessing of many women. Their adoring comments, sweet caresses, and bits of wisdom stand out in my memories of Enrichment Night.

Do we recognize in our own lives the opportunities for creation that are there? Do we prize the gifts, talents, and spirits God has given us? Do we share the creations of our hearts, minds, and hands with others? . . . We each have to say to ourselves, "What will I create of my life? My time? My future?" First, go where the Spirit directs. . . . Be patient, ask in faith, and you will receive guidance in your creative efforts. Second, don't be paralyzed from fear of making mistakes. . . . Don't be afraid. Do the best you can. Of course you will make mistakes. Everyone does. Learn from them and move forward. Third, support others along the way. Every person on this earth is unique. We all have varied interests, abilities, and skills. We are each at different levels physically, spiritually, and emotionally. Finally, rejoice. Creation isn't drudgery. Creation flows from love. When we do what we love, we rejoice along the way.

—Mary Ellen Smoot

✿

All of our sisters need stronger ties with one another in an environment that bolsters faith and strengthens families and supports struggles. Creating such a place with such opportunities is the work of Relief Society. And because every ward is different, there is no one-size-fits-all program. But there is the Spirit of the Lord for guidance, and charity, the pure love of Christ, which never faileth. What else do we need?!

—Bonnie D. Parkin

About the Author

A convert to the Church, Linda Hoffman Kimball lives in Evanston, Illinois, and holds a BA degree from Wellesley College and an MFA from Boston University. A columnist for the online interfaith magazine Beliefnet.com and for *Exponent II*, an LDS women's quarterly newspaper, Linda is also the author of two humorous novels for LDS adults—*Home to Roost* and *The Marketing of Sister B.* She edited and illustrated an essay collection by LDS writers, *Saints Well Seasoned: Musings on How Food Nourishes Us—Body, Heart and Soul* (Deseret Book, 1998).

Linda is an artist, poet, dog lover, and devoted wife to Christian E. Kimball and mother to three remarkable children. She is currently serving as the Relief Society President in the North Shore First Ward, Wilmette, Illinois Stake.